Contents

> 'Pride and Prejudice' is possibly the most read and most adapted of Jane Austen's novels.

Since the 'Jane Austen TV and Film Locations Guide' was published, four new adaptations of Austen's works have appeared. 'Mansfield Park', 'Persuasion' and 'Northanger Abbey' were shown as part of ITV's 'Jane Austen Season' in spring 2007, which included a re-airing of the 1996 production of 'Emma', and then, nine months later, 'Sense and Sensibility', another screenplay by Andrew Davies, was brought to our televisions by the BBC. On the big screen, 'Becoming Jane', which focused on the romantic possibilities of Jane's friendship with Tom Lefroy, was distributed by Miramax.

All productions of Jane Austen's six completed novels are characteristically different and fans have their own particular favourites. Similarly, each adaptation uses different locations,

and it is remarkable that sufficient Georgian architecture, stately homes and brooding castles survive to provide the variety of locations sought out by production designers and their teams. A few settings have been used several times, with Georgian Bath being an obvious example. Jane lived for a time in the town and large portions of two of her novels are set there. Repeated use of properties is not usual, though, and for the new adaptations the production teams found fresh locations in the south west of England and cast their nets wider, moving north to Yorkshire and over the sea to Ireland.

The right location is as important to the success of the costume drama as it is to the characters of Miss Austen's novels. Substantial properties feature in all of the books, and each plot presents a

man of good fortune with an impressive house to support. "About thirty years ago Miss Maria Ward, of Huntingdon, with only seven thousand pounds, had the good luck to captivate Sir Thomas Bertram, of Mansfield Park, in the county of Northampton, and to be thereby raised to the rank of a baronet's lady, with all the comforts and consequences of an handsome house and large income." The authenticity of less grand establishments, towns, villages and rural scenes are equally important to film makers and many places require 'makeovers' which creates difficulty in recognising the locations. This book is intended as a guide to the identification of locations that star in some screen productions of Jane Austen's novels.

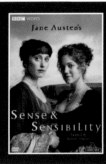

Sense and Sensibility 2008
BBC

Director: John Alexander
Screenplay: Andrew Davies

Starring:
Linda Bassett
Leo Bill
Lucy Boynton
Dominic Cooper
Janet McTeer
Hattie Morahan
David Morrissey
Claire Skinner
Charity Wakefield

A perfect combination...novel by Jane Austen, screenplay by Andrew Davies! The BBC got 2008 off to a fine start with this excellent three-part adaptation of the first of Jane Austen's novels to be published. 'Sense and Sensibility', written in 1797, was originally written under the title of the names of the two heroines, 'Elinor and Marianne', but when the novel was published anonymously by 'a Lady' in 1811, the book bore the title by which it is still known today.

The Locations

Barton Cottage
Blackpool Mill Cottage,
Hartland Abbey Estate, Devon

When Mrs. Dashwood's husband dies, she and her three daughters are obliged to leave their family home, Norland Park, to find accommodation elsewhere.

However, Mrs. Dashwood is of limited means, and must reduce her sights dramatically. She is gratified when a cottage belonging to her relation, Mr. John Middleton, becomes available.

Blackpool Mill at Hartland Abbey was picked to play the role of the Dashwood's humble new dwelling. Most of the interior scenes that took place at Barton Cottage were shot in studio, but the exterior was provided by 15th century Blackpool Cottage, which stands in a sheltered valley overlooking a bay washed by the Atlantic surf. Blackpool Mill was also used in the film of Rosamund Pilcher's 'The Shell Seekers'.

Barton Cottage Grounds
Coastal Footpath, Hartland Devon
(Sir Hugh Stucley)

The spectacular coastal scenes shown in the series were filmed on the Hartland Abbey estate, which includes five miles of unspoilt Atlantic coastline. Here Marianne roams in her abandoned misery.

Hartland Abbey was founded as an Augustinian monastery in 1157, but in 1539 at the Dissolution of the Monasteries, Henry VIII, obviously with regard to a very important service, gave the abbey to the Sergeant of his Wine Cellar. This lucky gentleman managed to keep his head, and the abbey remains in his family to this day.

Part of the gardens were lost in the undergrowth, but earlier this century, a Victorian fernery and paths laid out by Gertrude Jekyll were discovered. Woodland gardens, a bog garden and packed walled garden form part of a visit to the abbey.

> 'Sense and Sensibility' was originally written under the title of the names of the two heroines, 'Elinor and Marianne'

Delaford
Hall Barn, Beaconsfield,
Buckinghamshire

In order to smooth the course of true love, charming Colonel Brandon offers Edward Ferrars the living on his estate at Delaford. Edward and Elinor make their home at the rectory, while Colonel Brandon and his new wife, Elinor's sister, Marianne, take up residence nearby in the 'big house'!

Hall Barn was built in the seventeenth century for the poet, Edward Waller.

Waller had a near death experience when he was sent to the tower following the discovery of his plot, known as 'Waller's Plot', to oust the Parliamentary rebels. Waller pleaded for mercy, which he bought through bribes and betrayals of his fellow conspirators. He was fined £10,000 (hardly a drop in the ocean over three hundred years ago) and exiled. On his return to England in 1652 he wrote a poem to Cromwell; on the restoration of the king Waller changed his poetic sycophancy, to praise King Charles II. Samuel Johnson accused the poet of 'moral vacuity'!

Cleveland, The Palmer Estate
Ham House, Richmond, Surrey
(National Trust)

Said to be the most haunted house in England, Jacobean Ham House is a splendid Stuart mansion on the banks of the river at Richmond-upon-Thames. The house was built in 1610 for Sir Thomas Vavasour, Knight Marshal to James I. The Duchess of Lauderdale, who became mistress of the house some years later and is reputed to have murdered her husband, is said to walk through the house at night tapping her cane along the corridors. Many visitors to the house have reported seeing a ghostly cocker spaniel in the grounds.

Barton Park Exterior
Delaford Library
Loseley Park, Guildford
(Mr. Michael More-Molyneaux)

Loseley Park was built in the middle of the sixteenth century and is a fine example of Elizabethan architecture. Built by Sir William More to entertain the Queen, the house is still in the care of descendants of the More family. The collection of family paintings, furniture and tapestries has objects dating back to the early sixteenth century, and includes King George IV's coronation chair. Do look out for the remarkable drawing room fireplace, which is carved out of a single block of chalk. Parkland and gardens surround the house, there is an award winning rose garden planted with over one thousand bushes and the walled garden is laid out in the style of a Gertrude Jekyll design

Persuasion 2007
ITV
Director: Adrian Shergold
Producers: Rebecca Eaton
Murray Ferguson
Yvonne Isimeme
Ibazebo
David Snodin
Screenplay: Simon Burke

Starring: Sally Hawkins
Rupert Penry-Jones
Alice Krige
Anthony Head
Julia Davis
Michael Fenton
Stevens
Sam Hazeldine

The 1995 production of 'Persuasion' was a difficult act to follow, but this new version proved most agreeable and Rupert Penry-Jones, as a delectable Captain Wentworth, certainly cheered a Sunday evening!

The Locations

The obvious choice for some of the locations was the Assembly Rooms in Bath – more of which later – and the stunning Royal Crescent and Circus in Bath.

The Crescent, which was built to the Palladian designs of John Wood the Younger, and the exterior of Number One, which was the first house to be built in Royal Crescent, provided the exterior of Camden Place. The beautifully restored and authentically furnished house recreates a picture of fashionable life in Jane Austen's Bath. A tour includes the dining room, elegant drawing room, a bedroom designed for the Georgian lady and a kitchen displaying the paraphernalia of domestic life.

The location used for Anne Elliot's arrival in Bath is the Circus, and there are several panoramic shots of the area, including the scene where Anne runs frantically through Bath in search of Captain Wentworth.

Bath Street,
Bath

Transported back from the 21st to the 19th century, Bath Street was given a thorough makeover to create a bustling market scene. Geese cackled as they ran along the street, shoppers bargained in the market and the street was filled with chestnut sellers, horses, carriages, sedan chairs and pickpockets.

Great Chalfield Manor, Wiltshire

Uppercross Great House and Uppercross Cottage
Sheldon Manor, Chippenham, Wiltshire
(Private ownership)

The maturity of Sheldon Manor made it a perfect location for the interior and exterior of the home of the Musgrove families. The front elevation was used for the Musgroves Senior, and another elevation for the home of Charles and his family. This is Wiltshire's oldest inhabited manor house. The porch dates from the 13th century and there is a 15th century chapel and a garden with ancient yews, a mulberry tree and an abundance of old fashioned roses.

King Alfred the Great, 9th century ruler of Wessex, enjoyed hunting in the forests near Chippenham, which is a centuries old market town.

Meeting on the Beach
Seatown, Dorset

Captain Wentworth meets up with his friends, Captain James Benwick and Captain Harry Harville, on the beach at Seatown. Until around two hundred years ago, this was a hot spot for smugglers, but the illicit trade in these parts seems to have disappeared before Jane Austen's time. The long distance South West Coast Path runs above the beach under 'Golden Cap', which, as the highest point on the south coast, stands 619 feet above the sea. This is part of the Jurassic Coast – an ideal place for fossil hunters who may take a break from their endeavours at the Anchor Inn, which sits practically on the shingled beach.

Lyme Regis
Lyme Regis

Shortly after the demise of the Seatown smuggling, Lyme Regis came to the fore as one of the first resorts in the area. Jane Austen loved to holiday here, and it was in this delightful Dorset seaside town that she commenced her work, 'Persuasion'. It is to Lyme Regis that Captain Wentworth and his party go to spend time with Benwick and Harville. The real town of Lyme was used in this production and the earlier 1995 drama and in both Louisa Musgrove is seen jumping and falling from the actual Cobb. Amongst the contributions to the fame of Lyme are Drake's first skirmish with the Spanish Armada and the discovery, in 1811, by twelve-year-old Mary Anning of the fossilised ichthyosaurus about a mile along the shore.

Inn at Lyme Regis – Interior
Great Chalfield Manor, Wiltshire
(National Trust)

The 15th century Manor House near Melkenham is encircled by a moat and defensive wall. There is a colourful Arts and Crafts garden that was designed by Alfred Parsons, a noted English landscape painter, watercolourist and illustrator. His execution of high quality flower paintings and engravings took him into the field of garden design. At Chalfield Manor he included terraces, gazebos, lawns, roses and grass paths with views across the fishpond.

Kellynch - Sorry! This location must remain a mystery at the request of the owners.

Mansfield Park (2007)
Company Pictures

Director: Iain B MacDonald
Producer: Suzan Harrison
Screenplay: Maggie Wadey

Starring: Billie Piper
Hayley Atwell
James D'Arcy
Joseph Beattie
Michelle Ryan
Catherine Steadman
Blake Ritson
Jemma Redgrave
Douglas Hodge
Maggie O'Neill
Holly the Pug!

The Locations

Mansfield Park
Newby Hall, Ripon,
North Yorkshire (Mr. and Mrs.
Richard Compton)

> Looking for new locations, the film-makers ventured north into Yorkshire

Mansfield Park is the only setting from Jane Austen's novel to be shown in this television adaptation. All other locations in the book are brought into the drama through the recollections of the characters, negating the need for seaside slums as home for the Price family or rolling countryside for Fanny's drive to the Bertrams' stately residence.

Looking for new locations, the film-makers ventured north into Yorkshire where they discovered Newby Hall. In the thirteenth century, the property belonged to the Nubie family, who took their name from the place. By the late

seventeenth century, the house was in the ownership of Sir Edward Blackett, Member of Parliament for Ripon, who demolished the old house and built what is now the heart of Newby further up the slope away from the River Ure.

In 1748 Newby was sold to Richard Weddell who left it to his son, William. William was a leading light in the Society of Dilettanti, a group of gentlemen who took a passionate interest in the Ancient Greeks and Romans. In 1766 he returned from his Grand Tour with grand designs for Newby, and he engaged Robert Adam to transform the interior into neo-classical style,

7

Newby Hall gardens

fitting for the French tapestries and classical sculptures that he brought from Europe.

Visitors to the Hall can see the results of the great Scottish architect's work in the intricate plasterwork ceilings, friezes and panels that adorn the principal rooms, including the dining room and the library, which was originally the entrance hall. The Corinthian columns were brought from overseas along with the great tonnage of classical statuary housed in Adam's statue gallery, which he designed in the style of a Roman house. Don't miss the vast Roman sarcophagus made of white and purple marble or the statue of Venus.

A Victorian wing was added to the Hall by Robert de Grey Vyner and included a splendid staircase lit by Venetian gondola lamps. Robert's nephew, the 2nd Marquess of Ripon, was known to be one of the finest shots of his day, and a curious record of his 'bags' hangs at the top of the stairs. He reputedly recorded half a million kills in his life, including tigers, elephants and rhinoceros. There is a legendary story that he shot bees to keep his hand in when hunting was out of season!

The twenty-five acres of gardens at Newby are spectacular. A walk from the house takes in manicured lawns, long herbaceous borders, formal and compartment gardens. Water, rose, autumn and tropical gardens also feature as part of a meandering stroll that leads into woodland and back to the gardens. The Ure is at the bottom of the garden with pleasure boat rides along the gently flowing river.

The immaculate lawns caused a minor headache for the production crew, as they were just too well-mown for a Georgian garden. Cutting had to be suspended and the grass allowed to grow to a suitable length for the pre-petrol lawnmower era! Another external problem was created by the wrong sheep. The flock at Newby is a new breed, so the staffs' shepherding skills had to be brought into play to keep the newcomers out of shot. Other difficulties included noise from Darlington Dog Show, which transferred from a park in the nearby town, and aircraft from RAF Leeming. None of these difficulties were insurmountable, and apart from the occasional modern 'swiss-roll' hay bale, the grounds at Mansfield Park appear rooted in the nineteenth century.

The interior scenes were shot in some of the principal rooms.

The Tapestry Room

In this lavish room, young Fanny first met the Bertram family and Aunt Norris, and later the Crawford siblings were introduced. Subsequently, Miss Crawford is dismissed by a devastated Edmund.

The Library

The Library is first shown as Sir Thomas takes leave of his family, who take advantage of his absence to stage 'Lovers' Vows – a play in five acts' by Mrs. Inchbald. Henry Crawford becomes enamoured of Fanny as she plays hide-and-seek and runs off into the Statue Gallery. Sir Thomas sends Aunt Norris on her way, as she seeks to assist the recalcitrant Maria.

Newby Hall Library

The Dining Room

Host to several family meals and the delightful scene where Lady Bertram manoeuvres a private moment for Fanny and Edmund and then calls Sir Thomas to see the happy couple through the window.

Fanny's bedroom was built in a disused attic room. Here we see Edmund giving Fanny her birthday present, immediately dashing her hopes as he offers "A token of love from one of your oldest friends." It seems unlikely enough that Edmund would have been permitted access to a young girl's bedchamber, but Sir Bertram is also found here, haranguing Fanny because of her rejection of Mr. Crawford, and Edmund again appears when Fanny is preparing for bed.

The Print Bedroom

Over indulgent young Tom Bertram is brought home to recover or die in the Print Room. How could actor James D'Arcy manage to lie still while those slippery looking leeches were applied to his chest? In this room, Edmund kept watch and Fanny nursed and read to roguish young Tom.

Many scenes were shot in the garden including Fanny's birthday picnic, Edmund's proposal and Fanny and Edmund's wedding breakfast, where Lady Bertram spots the couple dancing a 'new dance' – the waltz. Although the waltz may be dated to a much earlier period in Europe, in England the dance was frowned upon. When the waltz was included in a London ball given by the Prince Regent in 1816, 'The Thunderer' had something to say about "the indecent foreign dance."

> "There is a legendary story that he shot bees to keep his hand in when hunting was out of season!"

Northanger Abbey (2007)
Across the Sea to Ireland

Director: Jon Jones
Producer: Keith Thompson
Screenplay: Andrew Davies

Starring: Felicity Jones
Michael Rudd
Liam Cunningham
Julia Dearden
Carey Mulligan
Gerry O'Brien
JJ Field
Sylvestra le Touzel
Desmond Barrit
William Beck
Catherine Walker

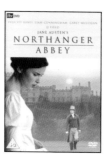

Jane Austen's young heroine, Catherine Morland, is taken to Bath by her wealthy friends, Mr. and Mrs. Allen. Forever dreaming of love and excitement, Catherine is an avid reader of Gothic novels and her rampant imagination projects her into all manner of compromising situations. In Bath she makes the acquaintance of suitable and unsuitable men and women, and her unworldly ways nearly cause her to be led astray.

About half of the drama is set in Bath, with the remaining part at Fullerton and Northanger Abbey. It is to Northanger that Catherine is invited by General Tilney, and in these Gothic surroundings her friendship with the General's daughter, Eleanor, and his younger son, Henry, grows. When the General finds that Catherine will inherit no fortune, she is dismissed in the dead of night and left to find her way home alone. All is well in the end, and Henry realises his love for Catherine and seeks her hand in marriage.

Dublin Castle

Lismore Castle

The Locations

Bath, Dublin Castle, Dublin
King's Inns, Henrietta Street,
Dublin

Various locations around Dublin were
used for the street and interior scenes that
took place in Bath.
Notable Georgian architecture may be
found at Henrietta and Bolton Streets.
The triumphal arch on Henrietta Street
was built in 1820 to hide the rather
awkward juxtaposition of the newly
constructed Kings' Inns, which had been
built on open fields and spoiled the vista
for the residents of Henrietta Street.

Dublin Castle is a large fortified complex
that was the seat of British rule in Ireland
until the early twentieth century. The
castle is now a major tourist attraction
and conference centre. Rooms open to the
public are St. Patrick's hall, the ballroom,
the Viceregal Apartments and the Throne
Room, which contains the throne from
the seventeenth century reign of King
William III.

Northanger Abbey
Lismore Castle, Lismore, County
Waterford

There can have been no disappointment
for Catherine Morland in this version
of 'Northanger Abbey'. All her darkest, most
erotic dreams and fantasies might have
been fulfilled within the walls of Lismore
Castle, which looms large and louring
above the River Blackwater.

Although a castle is not an abbey, the site
does have an ecclesiastical architectural
link as a monastery, founded in 633, once
stood on the site. The castle in its time has
belonged to King John, Sir Walter Raleigh
and Richard Boyle, the first Earl of Cork.
The Duke of Devonshire, whose
Derbyshire house, Chatsworth, was used
in the 2005 version of 'Pride and
Prejudice', is the property's current owner.

11

Becoming Jane (2007)
Ecosse Films in association
with Blueprint Productions

Director: Julian Jarrold
Producers: Graham Broadbent
                Robert Bernstein
                Douglas Rae
Screenplay: Kevin Hood and
                Sarah Williams

Starring: Anne Hathaway
                James McAvoy
                Julie Walters
                James Cromwell
                Dame Maggie Smith
                Ian Richardson

Fact has been married to
fiction to produce a love story
that may be seen as a basis
for 'Pride and Prejudice'

When Jon Spence was writing his recent
biography of Jane Austen, he looked more
deeply into the details surrounding her 1795
meeting with Tom Lefroy. 'Becoming Jane' is
based on facts unearthed in Spence's research
that indicate a romantic link between the
English novelist and Tom, a trainee
Irish lawyer, when they were both aged twenty.
Fact has been married to fiction to produce a
love story that may be seen as a basis for 'Pride
and Prejudice'. All filming for the production
took place in Ireland.

Steventon Rectory, Jane's Childhood Home
Higginsbrook House, near Trim, County Meath (Private ownership)

Higginsbrook was built in 1747 just outside the small town of Trim (starred in the film 'Braveheart'). The house appears larger from the outside than it actually is, and creates a perfect air of assumed grandness. Inside the house was 'de-modernised', and outside additions were made, including accommodation for domestic livestock. Washing appears to be becoming a feature of Jane Austen productions, as yards of sheets are shown blowing in the wind. The family who own Higginsbrook appeared as extras in the film and managed to round up well over a hundred friends and acquaintances for a crowd scene.

Exterior and Interior of Home of Lady Gresham
Killruddery House, Bray, County Wicklow (The Earls of Meath)

Located about twelve miles south of Dublin, Killruddery has been home to the Brabazon family (Earls of Meath) since 1618. The style is of the Elizabethan Revival, remodelled in the early nineteenth century but reduced in the 1950s.

The very large gardens are the last remaining in Ireland which still survive in their seventeenth century design.

Dublin City Hall

13

Charleville Castle

The house has an orangery through which guests pass when they attend Lady Gresham's ball.

Charleville Castle, Tullamore, County Offaly (Charleville Castle Heritage Trust)

As if by magic, when Lady Gresham's guests reach the other side of the Orangery, they find themselves no longer in Killruddery House, but in Charleville Castle. The castle is the finest example of Gothic-Revival architecture in Ireland.

The Ballroom
Dublin's City Hall

Built in the latter part of the eighteenth century, the City Hall, on the corner of Dame Street and Parliament Street, is a fine example of Georgian architecture, for which Dublin is renowned. The quality of the Georgian buildings played a part in the decision to film 'Becoming Jane' in Ireland, along with the smaller, low hedged fields that are typical of Jane Austen's era, and significant tax advantages that encourage filming in Ireland. The ball was held in the fabulous rotunda, which has recently been returned to its original design.

Steventon Rectory
Cloghlee Bridge

When the Reverend Austen delivers his cautionary sermon, the pulpit from which he lectures is far away from Hampshire in the hills outside Dublin at a little church dedicated to St. John the Baptist. The River Liffey rises nearby in the Sally Gap in the Wicklow Hills and flows a short way to pass the churchyard, meandering its seventy-five mile route out to sea, gathering up water courses as it passes, including a small stream that flows from the churchyard. The church was built in 1833 – a little modern for Jane Austen – but the superb setting amongst the fields lent itself to the film-makers' requirements. Several scenes were shot outside, and at the end of the film a bridal couple are shown. The scene where the groom throws his hat in the air was shot several times. For Austen aficionados who would like a tranquil stay in the area, Kippure House Estate has a very friendly staff who can direct them to the church.

Regency London
Henrietta Street and King's Inn, Dublin

The well preserved Georgian architecture again enticed the film makers.

Edward's House by the Sea

The house was built as a set and transported to a car park overlooking the beach at Donabate in County Dublin.

Working Title Films 2005		Starring:	Keira Knightley
			Matthew Macfadyen
Director:	Joe Wright		Brenda Blethyn
Producers:	Tim Bevan		Donald Sutherland
	Eric Fellner		Jena Malone
	Paul Webster		Dame Judi Dench
Screenplay:	Deborah Moggach		Rosamund Pike

" The story begs to be taken from the page to the big screen "

'Pride and Prejudice', the much loved story of misunderstanding born of class prejudices and the subsequent triumph of love, is possibly the most read and most adapted of Jane Austen's novels.

The story begs to be taken from the page to the big screen. Nonetheless, sixty-five years elapsed between the 1940 MGM Production starring Lawrence Olivier and Greer Garson, and the 2005 Working Title production with Keira Knightley and Matthew Macfadyen.

Basildon Park

The Locations

Roughly In Order of Appearance

Longbourn,
the Bennet Family Home
Groombridge Place,
Tunbridge Wells, Kent
(Private Ownership)

'Pride and Prejudice' devotees would never expect the Bennet house to be quiet, and indeed the only peace to be found by the sisters' long suffering father was in his personal domain, the library, where feminine intrusion was most unwelcome: "I shall be glad to have the library to myself as soon as possible." Groombridge Place was between owners at the time of filming, which was helpful in allowing the production company to make some major changes to fit the period in which the film is set. This late

17th century manor house was transformed to what the film makers describe as "late 18th century shabby chic" Externally the windows were changed to fit the period whilst the courtyard was transformed from tidy to muddy farmyard, complete with pigs, chickens and acre upon acre of billowing white washing. The house is moated and a duckboard bridge was built across the water for scenes with Elizabeth.

Whilst there is no public access to the house, award-winning Groombridge Place Gardens and Enchanted Forest (Groombridge Asset Management) are open for much of the year. First laid out in 1674 the formal walled gardens are set against a backdrop of the moat. Included in the many attractions are a secret garden, herbaceous borders, Paradise Walk and the Drunken Garden which features crazy topiary.

Netherfield Park,
Mr. Bingley's Country Residence
Basildon Park,
Lower Basildon, Reading, Berkshire
(National Trust)

The excitement at Longbourn when the females of the Bennet family discover that Netherfield Park is to be rented by "a young man of large fortune from the North of England" knows no bounds. Any wonder when five young Bennet sisters need husbands to give them security and status, their own home being entailed to the odious Mr. Collins!

Basildon Park is an 18th century classical house designed by Carr of York and set in four hundred acres of parkland. Rescued from impending dereliction in the middle of the last century, fine plasterwork, pictures and furniture are to be seen inside. The unusual octagonal

Stamford in costume

Burghley House, Stamford

drawing room, where Miss Bingley and Miss Bennett take a turn about the room whilst teasing poor Mr. Darcy, the dining room and the sumptuous ballroom star in the film. When the house is seen 'being put to bed' after Mr. Bingley departs for London, teams of white-gloved footmen are shown through the loggia doors sheeting all the furniture.

Meryton Town
Stamford, Lincolnshire

Proclaimed as 'The Finest Stone Town In England', this description would seem perfectly fitting. Stamford oozes charm from every pore. Streets wind and bend, small squares, beautiful churches and Georgian architecture are around every corner.

The town remains largely unspoilt. For over three hundred years much of the

land around Stamford was controlled by Lord Burghley and his descendants and was prevented from developing and expanding. When the Great Northern Line was built in 1844, the new rail service bypassed Stamford, stopping at Peterborough instead. Stamford's coaching trade collapsed, leaving the town with an economic disaster.

Stamford has also largely escaped the familiar modern day homogenisation of its town centre and environs. The town's exceptional character was recognised by the Royal Commission on Historic Monuments in the 1960s and was made the first conservation area in England.

Despite the preservation of the town it still took the film's production team six weeks to transform Stamford into Meryton of the 1790s, including covering huge ground sheets with tons of soil and

sand to replicate 18th century streets. A false frontage was built across the bottom of Maiden Lane to form a butcher's shop, a portico was added and doors and windows altered at the Arts Centre in St. Mary's Street.

Many local people were used as extras and four hundred 'militia' marched through the town, the 'soldiers' members of a Napoleonic Society.

Amongst its other film credits, Stamford has starred in 'Middlemarch' (BBC 1993), 'The War of the Stones' (Amateur Film 2004), 'Blue Sky' (Image Productions 2002) and 'The Golden Bowl' (Merchant Ivory 2001).

St. Peter's Church, Brooke

Rosings, Home of Lady Catherine de Bourgh
Burghley House, Stamford, Lincolnshire
(Burghley House Preservation Trust Ltd)

This grand Elizabethan house might have overwhelmed a less strong-minded girl than Miss Elizabeth Bennet when visiting the regal Lady Catherine, Mr. Darcy's dowager aunt, and patron of Mr. Collins.

Burghley is one of the largest houses in England still in the ownership of the descendants of the family who built it. Constructed in the late 16th century for Sir William Cecil, 1st Lord Burghley, who was advisor and Lord Treasurer to Queen Elizabeth I, it presents a magnificent sight from every approach.

The Elizabethan exterior remains almost as it was when built in the days of 'Good Queen Bess', but the interior was remodelled in the 17th century. This fine house sits in a 300-acre deer park designed by Capability Brown who was also responsible for some of the internal alterations made by John, the 5th Earl of Exeter, who established an extensive collection of art treasures at the house. Take the tour to see the stunning work of Antonio Verrio in the 'Heaven' room, used as Lady Catherine's drawing room. Other parts of the house were used for interior and exterior scenes at Rosings, and members of the Burghley staff played Rosings' butlers and footmen.

There is a strangely fascinating display of turtle skulls in the kitchen. These poor creatures will have been brought alive from foreign parts to be made into turtle soup. The kitchen also displays 260 Georgian and Victorian copper utensils and a life-size painting by Frans Snyders of a 'Butchered Ox'.

Mr. Collin's Church at Hunsford
St. Peter's Church, Brooke, Near Oakham, Rutland

Recognised as Sir John Betjeman's favourite smallest church, it is easy to see why the filmmakers chose this lovely buiding in this pretty hamlet, although only the interior was used in the filming. A grassy path leads from a gate through the churchyard to the door, or leads on out of the grounds through a second gate. There is a low thirteenth century tower and much of the interior is Elizabethan. Light streams through the clear windows onto the stone flagged floor and the aisle is off-centre running between rows of box pews. This most tranquil setting merits a visit, and do take a look in the visitors' book and read what a member of the film crew had to say.

Pemberley Exterior, Fitzwilliam Darcy's family home
Chatsworth House, Bakewell, Derbyshire
(Trustees of the Chatsworth Settlement. Home of the Duke and Duchess of Devonshire)

"The eye was instantly caught by Pemberley House". It is possible that Jane Austen modelled Mr. Darcy's Pemberley on the 'Great Treasure House of Chatsworth', which stands magnificent in parkland and 105 acres of gardens. Legend has it that the author visited the neighbouring town of Bakewell, possibly spending some time at the town's Rutland Arms Hotel, although this has never been verified. Lizzie Bennet and the Gardiners start their tour of Pemberley at the grand staircase in the Painted Hall, and in the Sculpture Gallery Elizabeth admires rather lingeringly, the bust of Mr. Darcy whilst listening to his housekeeper's flattering description of our hero.

Built by Bess of Hardwick in 1552, Chatsworth House has been lived in by the Cavendish family, the Dukes of Devonshire ever since. On a visit to Chatsworth, the tour takes in twenty-six rooms, including five 17th century staterooms that have been little changed. Painted ceilings by Antonio Verrio, Sir James Thornhill and Louis Laguerre, paintings by Rembrandt, Tintoretto and Landseer, tapestries and a dazzling silver collection are but a few of the treasures to be viewed in the house. The grounds are stunning, from the two hundred metre cascade to the rockeries and glasshouses designed by Joseph Paxton. The story is told that the gardeners were on to a good thing and knew how to enjoy themselves – the pipe from the brewhouse ran down through one of the greenhouses, and not all of the beer made it as far as the house!

Matthew Macfadyen at Wilton House, The Interior for Pemberley

Pemberley Interior
Wilton House, Near Salisbury
(The Earl of Pembroke)

Pemberley, home of Mr. Darcy – "The rooms were lofty and handsome and their furniture suitable to the fortune of their proprietor." So mused Miss Elizabeth Bennet as she looked around the great house with her aunt and uncle Mr. and Mrs. Gardiner. "And of this place," thought she, "I might have been mistress."

The magnificent interior of Wilton House, the ancestral home of the Earl of Pembroke and his family for 450 years, provided a perfect location for some of the interior scenes in Mr. Darcy's home. Miss Elizabeth is seen wandering dreamily through the rooms, discovering, to her horror, that Mr. Darcy is at home.

Here Elizabeth meets Georgiana, Darcy's sister, who greets first her brother, and then her future sister-in-law, with warm affection.

Visitors to the house are treated to one of the finest displays of art in Europe with paintings on show by Rubens, Van Dyck and Brueghel, Greek and Roman statuary and a lock of Queen Elizabeth I's hair. Although only the interior was used in the film, don't miss out on the beautiful gardens. The house stands in landscaped parkland and there are four new gardens created since 1969 by the 17th Earl of Pembroke.

Of further interest to filmgoers is the use of Wilton House in the making of the films 'The Madness of King George', 'Mrs. Brown' and 'Sense and Sensibility' – more of which later.

Derbyshire Tour
Stanage Edge, Hathersage Moor,
Derbyshire

On meeting Mr. Darcy as she viewed Pemberley with her aunt and uncle, Elizabeth covers her confusion with inconsequential talk: "She wanted to talk, but there seemed an embargo on every subject. At last she recollected that she had been travelling, and they talked of Matlock and Dove Dale with great perseverance". In this production, Miss Elizabeth Bennet takes in the beauty of the Derbyshire Dales from Stanage Edge, the largest and most impressive of the grit stone edges. The Edge runs about three and a half miles from Stanage End in the north to Cowper Stone in the south and is crossed by Long Causeway, the Roman road that ran from Navio (Brough) to Danum (Doncaster).

Haddon Hall

Stanage Edge

Follow in Keira Knightley's steps with a walk to Stanage Edge and blow the cobwebs away, or merely observe its grandeur from miles away in the Hope Valley.

The Inn at Lambton and Miss Elizabeth Bennet's Bedroom
Haddon Hall, Bakewell, Derbyshire (Lord Edward Manners)

Haddon Hall took two starring roles in this film. The Banqueting Hall played the Inn at Lambton and the Dining Hall starred as Elizabeth Bennet's bedroom at Longbourn.

There has been a dwelling at Haddon since the 11th century, but the present house was built in the 14th century with two hundred years of additions and further alterations in the 17th century, which included the building of the Long Gallery. The Hall, which is built on a rocky outcrop, was abandoned for two hundred years and missed out on 17th and 18th century architectural changes. Consequently it still looks much as it would have during Tudor times when Henry VIII's brother, Arthur, often visited the Vernons, who owned the house.

Visitors to Haddon may also enjoy the terraced gardens where over one hundred and fifty varieties of rose and clematis grow, many established for over seventy years.

Haddon was also used as a location in 'Elizabeth' and 'Jane Eyre'.

Rosings Garden
Temple of Apollo, Stourhead Gardens, Stourton, Wiltshire (National Trust)

In the beautiful setting of The Temple of Apollo, in the pouring rain, Mr. Darcy proposes, and is refused by Elizabeth who makes her escape across the Palladian Bridge. Keira Knightley does full justice to Elizabeth's impassioned rejection speech, leaving Matthew Macfadyen's Mr. Darcy with the wind taken out of his sails.

The beautiful 18th century landscaped garden was laid out by Henry Hoare II. The two classical temples – The Pantheon and The Temple of Apollo – are set around a central lake. As visitors move around the lake through the mature woodland they are treated to changing views of the buildings

Musical Instruments
Finchcocks Living Museum of Music, Goudhurst, Kent

Musical ability (or lack of it in poor Mary Bennet's case) features prominently in Jane Austen's novels. It follows then, that musical instruments would be required as props in the films. Several instruments were provided for 'Pride and Prejudice' by Finchcocks Living Museum of Music in Kent.

Finchcocks is a Georgian manor, where the magnificent Richard Burnett collection of historical keyboard instruments is housed. The collection includes seventy pianos from the late 18th and early 19th centuries, harpsichords, clavichords and, the oldest instrument in the collection, the Italian virginal that was made in 1668 by Guarracino.

Finchcocks also supplied instruments for the 1996 film of 'Emma' and the 1995 film of 'Sense and Sensibility'.

Finchcocks Living Museum of Music

Grand Piano by Muzio Clementi & Co, London, c.1815. From the Finchcocks Collection

Mansfield Park 1999
BBC/Miramax Feature Film

Director: Patricia Rozema
Producer: Sarah Curtis
Screenplay: Patricia Rozema

Starring: Frances O'Connor
Harold Pinter
Jonny Lee Miller
Embeth Davitz
Hugh Bonneville
Alessandro Nivola

The Locations

This production of 'Mansfield Park' was based on the novel of that name published in 1814, and Jane Austen's letters and early writings.

Fanny Price is niece of Sir Thomas and Lady Bertram of Mansfield Park. Lady Bertram's sister, having married for love rather than money and status, found herself living in Portsmouth, married to her 'love', an uneducated and unconnected Lieutenant of Marines who is now an invalid. Fanny's mother struggles to cope with her growing – in both senses - family and in desperation resumes contact with the Lady Bertram and her other sister, Aunt Norris.

Portsmouth

The film opens in the Price family home on the quayside in Portsmouth, which is shown when Fanny Price, nominated by her mother to live ostensibly with her Aunt Norris, is seen leaving her home and entering the coach that will take her to Mansfield Park.

Coastal Views
Charlestown, Cornwall and Weymouth and Lulworth Cove, Dorset

As young Fanny is driven by coach and horses to Northampton, the film's audience is treated to panoramic shots of the sea and beautiful coastline. Riding high along the route of the South West Coast long distance footpath the beauty of the Dorset coastline is there for all to see.

MANSFIELD PARK

Mansfield Park
The Bertrams' House
Kirby Hall, Deene, Corby,
Northamptonshire (National Trust)

Set down at daybreak in front of the imposing entrance to Mansfield Park, Fanny is greeted by a drunken porter atop the gatehouse, and then left to wait for two hours until the arrival of her Aunt Norris.

Cast in the role of Mansfield Park, Kirby Hall just takes the breath away. Tranquilly set near an unclassified road off the A43 Corby to Stamford route, approaching this Elizabethan treasure is a joy. Largely ruined, parts of the interior remain and are undergoing painstaking restoration. Light streams through the Elizabethan bay windows and it is easy to imagine the house in its early glory.

Kirby Hall looms in the semi-darkness over the diminutive figure of the young Fanny Price standing against the backdrop of the imposing entrance gates. She is ushered into the Great Hall by her Aunt Norris where Fanny meets some of her relations – the overbearing Sir Thomas and opium befuddled Lady Bertram. Sent from the room while her fate is discussed, Fanny meets the two Bertram daughters descending the stone staircase into the inner hall.

The Great Hall is used to effect in 'Mansfield Park'. The high ceiling and minstrels gallery' dwarfing Fanny. Later in the film, the hall is transformed into a magnificent ballroom for the ball, which Sir Thomas holds in Fanny's honour, and the Gallery was used for musicians. A large part of the action was shot at Kirby Hall, and the makers of the film made great use of the leaded Elizabethan windows, shooting through them from within and without. Some scenes have been shot from the exterior, where the camera moves from top to bottom of the huge bay windowed west front of the house, showing different enactments in each of the windows.

The filming at Kirby Hall took place in 1998 and lasted six weeks. During shooting of the 'Ball Scene' there were thirty members of the film crew and two hundred extras, not to mention the ninety vehicles.

The bow windowed parlour was the setting for the drawing room at Mansfield Park, whilst the bow windowed great bedchamber became the setting for Maria's bedroom.

Exterior scenes were shot in the garden, which has been reconstructed as a parterre. Formal gardens such as these were designed to be enjoyed outside as well as viewed from within the house, providing pleasure during the colder months.

Sir Humphrey Stafford commenced the building of Kirby Hall in 1570 and the magnificent property was completed by Sir Christopher Hatton, a favourite of Queen Elizabeth I's. Many of the large Elizabethan houses were built in eager hope of a visit from the Queen on her annual 'progresses' around England, but there is no conclusive evidence that the Queen ever visited Kirby. Royalty was however received, when James I visited in 1619.

Time at Kirby just slips away, as you start your tour in the forecourt, enter the impressive loggia and go beyond to the inner forecourt and the beautiful remains.

Kirby Hall - Mansfield Park

> "This production of 'Mansfield Park' was based on the novel published in 1814, and Jane Austen's letters and early writings."

Visit To A Stately Home
Osterley Park House, Jersey Road, Isleworth, Middlesex (National Trust)

Originally built in 1575, Osterley Park was transformed in the 18th century by architect Robert Adam.

The mansion has a classical interior with impressive plasterwork and original tapestries, paintings and furniture. There is a huge 16th century stable block, which is still used.

Gardens
Kenwood House, Hampstead, London (English Heritage)

Some of the garden scenes were shot at Kenwood House, which stands in one hundred and twelve acres of landscaped grounds on the edge of Hampstead Heath. The grounds were also used in the film 'Notting Hill'. Here is another house remodelled by Robert Adam, the 18th century neo-classical architect. One of his greatest achievements is the Great Room at Kenwood. The house is famous for its important collection of paintings that were bequeathed to the nation by Edward Guinness. Works by Rembrandt, Vermeer, Gainsborough, Turner and Reynolds are on display here.

Osterley Park House

Kenwood House Grounds

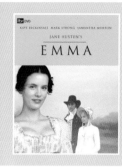

Emma 1996
Meridian – ITV/A & E Television
Movie

Director: Diarmuid Lawrence
Producer: Sue Birtwistle
Screenplay: Andrew Davies

Starring:

Kate Beckinsale
Mark Strong
Bernard Hepton
Samantha Bond
Prunella Scales
James Hazeldine
Dominic Rowan
Samantha Morton

The Locations

Two versions of 'Emma' were produced in a year. This television version, with a screenplay by Andrew Davies, writer of the previous year's BBC dramatisation of 'Pride and Prejudice', gave the truer picture of the two of life in the early 1800s. There were real contrasts between the lifestyles of people with and those without money. Director Diarmuid Lawrence has captured the period with the authenticity of the muddy roads, the food, the dirty interiors and the servants' 'invisible' role. People with money were so indolent, it is no wonder Emma had time on her hands to interfere in other people's love lives for her own entertainment.

Donwell Abbey

Three properties were used as the setting for Mr. Knightley's impressive home. One of the most human and down to earth scenes was the harvest supper where everyone let their hair down and mixed together. Note the lovely black Labrador joining in the supper in front of Emma and Mr. Knightley.
This took place in...

The Great Hall,
Broughton Castle,
Banbury, Oxfordshire
(Lord and Lady Saye and Sele)

Broughton Castle is the family home of Lord and Lady Saye and Sele. Built in the 1300s, it stands on an island surrounded by a huge moat. Much of the medieval manor

house still remains, but the castle was enlarged at the end of the 16th century at which time magnificent plaster ceilings, panelling and fireplaces were added. In the 17th century William, the 8th Lord Saye and Sele, opposed Charles I in his efforts to rule without Parliament, and Broughton became a secret meeting place for the King's opponents.

The gardens are mixed herbaceous borders planted with many old roses and there is a formal walled garden. Visitors are welcome to see the gatehouse and parkland as well as the 14th century Church of St. Mary

Donwell Abbey Exteriors
Sudeley Castle, Winchcombe, Nr. Cheltenham, Gloucestershire (Lord and Lady Ashcombe)

Visitors looking to follow in the path of Royalty while on their Jane Austen tour should definitely include Sudeley. Home of Lord and Lady Ashcombe and the Dent-Brocklehurst family, Sudeley is one of the great historic houses and dates back one thousand years. Once the property of King Ethelred the Unready, much later it was the home of Katherine Parr, sixth wife of Henry VIII. Henry VIII, Ann Boleyn, Lady Jane Grey and Elizabeth I all visited, and King Charles I stayed here, his nephew, Prince Rupert, establishing it as his headquarters during the Civil War.

In the 19th century Sudeley was restored for new owners, the Dent brothers, who largely refurnished the house from pieces bought at the contents sale of Hugh Walpole's house at Strawberry Hill. The castle is surrounded by award-winning gardens that are famous for their topiary, old-fashioned roses, the Secret Garden and the Tudor knot garden.

Donwell Abbey Interiors
Stanway House and Water Garden, Stanway, Winchcombe, Gloucestershire (Lord Neidpath)

World records here at Stanway with the magnificent fountain in the restored water garden – one of the finest in Britain. Reaching over three hundred feet, this is the tallest gravity fountain in the world and the second tallest fountain in Europe. Stanway is a pretty manor house in a sheltered Cotswold location. Most of the furniture has been in the house since it was built and the charming interior feels like a home rather than a museum. Specimen trees, avenues and parkland and a 14th century tithe barn complete the visit.

The magnificent fountain at Stanway House

Trafalgar House

Lacock

Dorney Court

Thame Park House

Hartfield
Trafalgar House, Wiltshire
(Private Ownership)

Home of Mr. Woodhouse and his scheming daughter, Emma. Mr. Woodhouse worries and sleeps his days away, as Emma, with far too much money and time on her hands, schemes and plots marriages for others, ignoring the truth of where her own heart lies.

Trafalgar House was given to Lord Nelson's family by the government.

Highbury
Lacock, Wiltshire (National Trust)

This charming little town has many lime-washed, half-timbered and stone houses, as well as Lacock Abbey and the Fox Talbot Museum, a memorial to the man who lived in the village and invented the modern photographic negative.

The village still resembles a medieval town in part, with houses from the 13th century, but virtually no building from after the 18th century. This makes Lacock a popular location for production companies and the village counts amongst its television and film credits 'Moll Flanders', 'Pride and Prejudice', 'Harry Potter' and 'Emma', which was shot partly in Church Street.

Randalls
Dorney Court, Windsor, Berkshire
(The Palmer Family)

Mr. and Mrs. Weston live in newly wedded bliss in this fine Tudor manor house. The house, of 'outstanding architectural and historical importance', lies just outside Windsor. The Palmer family have lived here for 450 years and visitors gain a rare insight into how the squirearchy lived over half a millennium ago. The house has a magnificent great hall and a collection of family portraits, oak and lacquer furniture, needlework and panelled rooms. The 13th century church has a Norman font and Tudor tower.

Abbey Mill Farm: Gypsy Camp: Hartfield Interiors: Strawberry Beds: The Sea off Weymouth
Thame Park, Oxfordshire
(Private Ownership)

These 18th century pleasure gardens are on the site of a Cistercian Abbey, which was listed as the third richest Cistercian house in England at the Dissolution of the Monasteries. Many features from the abbey were built into Thame Park House, which is privately owned.

Thame Park is the location of the Martins' home, Abbey Mill Farm, where young Robert Martin pines for Miss Smith, who has been advised against such a marriage by the scheming, match-making Emma.

The derelict walled garden was cleared and tidied for the scene where the characters go strawberry picking. This strawberry picking party provided one of the most amusing scenes in this version of 'Emma', with the dreadful Mrs. Elton's whimsical imaginings of herself as a shepherdess: "I fancy myself as a sort of shepherdess" and Miss Bates - delightfully played by Prunella Scales - response "Oh! Are you fond of sheep then, Mrs. Elton?" This 'back to nature' leisure pursuit of the party offered further entertainment value with the imperious waving of hands at the long suffering footmen, methodically moving the kneeling cushions along the rows of strawberries for the picking party.

Believe it or not, the storm beleaguered boat scene at Weymouth was shot in an Oxfordshire Field at Thame Park!

Box Hill
A Hill In the Chilterns

The picnic at Box Hill brought many of the characters together, allowing a good perspective of their personalities and the interplay between them, but one of the overriding memories of the scene in this film was the journey. A procession of horses, carts and carriages carried the provisions, crockery, glasses, cutlery, tables, umbrellas, servants and picnickers with serving girls clinging onto the side of the carts for dear life as they rumbled and trundled their way up the hill. Such a shame after all that effort that Emma so selfishly spoiled the day!

Emma 1996
Miramax Feature film

Director: Douglas McGrath
Producers: Patrick Cassavetti
Steven Haft
Screenplay: Douglas McGrath

Starring:

Gwyneth Paltrow
Jeremy Northam
Toni Collette
James Cosmo
Greta Scaachi
Alan Cumming

Locations

The Miramax film takes a more lighthearted approach to Jane Austen's novel, which she wrote in 1814/15, with Gwyneth Paltrow playing the scheming Emma.

Real life mother and daughter, Phyllida Law and Sophie Thompson (sister of Academy Award winning actress Emma Thompson) play screen mother and daughter, Mrs. Bates and spinster Miss Bates.

Lizzie the pig, starred alongside one of her owners from The Rare Poultry and Pig Centre at Milton Abas. An Oxford Sandy and Black, sometimes known as the 'plum pudding pig', she was one of the rarest breeds. Unfortunately the centre is no longer open to the public, but if a rare pig is required, this is the place to go. Lizzie had done well at many shows and came to stardom as a well-trained performer!

Highbury
Evershot

Transformed into the village of Highbury for the film, Evershot lies where the River Frome rises from a spring at St. John's Well. This small village is in the hills, and is one of the highest villages in Dorset. Raised pavements line the main street, and the shops have bow fronted windows. This pretty little village is surrounded by unspoilt landscape which adds to its timeless charm.

Milton Abbas

The 'new' village of Milton Abbas also provided scenes for the film…as well as Lizzie the Pig. The village is now a hillside street of thatched cottages, a row of 18th century almshouses and St. James' church.

31

Until the 18th century, there was a town at Milton Abbas that had grown up around the 10th century abbey. The whole town was demolished in 1780 by Joseph Damer, the 1st Earl of Dorchester, because he felt it was too close to his house. The five-year-old son of the previous owner demonstrated the wisdom of the fashion for dressing male children in petticoats, when he fell from the top of the sixty-foot church tower, parachuting to the ground to survive until nearly ninety years of age!

The great Capability Brown, employed by the first Earl, designed the 'new' village, where all the people who had not been driven away were rehoused. Most of the old village is under the lake, including the property of one indomitable villager who on refusing to move, was flooded out, later winning his case against the Earl in court.

In 1309 the abbey was struck by lightning, causing a fire which destroyed all the buildings and documents. The present church, built in the 14th and 15th centuries, was restored by Sir George Gilbert Scott in the latter part of the nineteenth century.

The house is now an independent school, but the church is open for visitors, and the surrounding countryside is beautiful.

Churches

Several churches featured in the film. One of particular note and well worth a visit is St. Michael and All Angels, East Coker, Somerset.

William Dampier one of the first Englishmen to see Australia, was born in East Coker in 1651 and in the same century, the ancestors of T.S. Eliot left for New England. Eliot immortalised the village in his poem 'East Coker', the second of his Four Quartets. T.S. Eliot arranged to have his ashes buried in East Coker church where his ancestor, Andrew Eliot had been baptised in 1627, thereby fulfilling the first line of the poem: "In my beginning is my end." There is a memorial to Eliot, and another to William Dampier who became a pirate, adventurer and explorer, landing in Western Australia in 1688 – nearly one hundred years before Captain Cook landed in Botany Bay.

Coker Court, East Coker, Somerset

Coker Court is a Manor House dating from the 15th century. The building is listed, but has been divided to make multiple homes and is in private ownership.

People have lived on the site since Roman times, including the mother of King Harold II, Gytha Thorgilsson wife of Godwin, Earl of Wessex, who died at the battle of Hastings.

'Emma' fans can take in the beautiful Somerset countryside and enjoy quiet reflection in this interesting small church.

St. Michael and All Angels, East Coker

Donwell Abbey
the Ballroom Scene
Claydon House, Middle Claydon, Nr. Buckingham (National Trust)

The ball was filmed at this striking 18th century country house. A beautiful scene is shot through the windows as Mr. Knightley talks with Emma on the terrace. Mr. Elton is yet another curate to be given harsh treatment by Jane Austen, when he shows the extent of his class consciousness at the ball where he rudely snubs poor Harriet Smith who is rescued by the charming Mr. Knightley.

Florence Nightingale was a relative of the Verney family who lived at Claydon House. She was a frequent visitor and part of the tour of the house includes the bedroom that she used. The house is 18th century, located in parkland looking out over a lake. Relics of the exploits of the Verney family in the English Civil War are on display and there is a series of great rooms with wood-carvings in Chinese and Gothic styles. Claydon House was also used in the making of William Makepeace Thackeray's 'Vanity Fair'.

Weddings, Puppies and Pergolas
Mapperton, Beaminster, Dorset (The Earl and Countess of Sandwich)

Mapperton House and Gardens, a beautiful Jacobean manor, is located in an area of outstanding natural beauty. The Italianate garden, topiary, shrub gardens, formal gardens and fishponds provide beautiful surroundings for relaxing strolls. All Saints Church is attached to the house and opens onto the courtyard.

Filming for 'Emma' took place in the gardens and ancillary buildings, including the front courtyard, where filming for Emma's marriage to Mr. Knightley took place. Harriet Smith is seen with Emma in the North Stable Block playing with a litter of spaniel puppies, and filming also took place in a pergola in the garden. Mapperton featured in the BBC Television adaptation of Henry Fielding's novel, 'Tom Jones'.

Stafford House, West Stafford, Dorset (Private Ownership)

Built in 1633 and extended in the 19th century, Stafford House is now in private ownership.

The virtually unchanged village of West Stafford featured in Thomas Hardy's novel, 'Tess of the d'Urbervilles' – she married Angel Clare in the church here. Thatched rooves abound – even the bus shelter is thatched. The fortified house, Woodsford Castle, is nearby. Mainly 14th century, the house is believed to be one of England's largest thatched buildings.

Box Hill
Location Unconfirmed

Stunning Dorset countryside a likely candidate!

That famous picnic again! Strawberry picking and picnicking were combined into one scene in this film. Emma's barbed rebuke of Miss Bates so painful, and the uncomfortable discomposure of Miss Bates performed by Sophie Thompson so palpable as it's enough to make the audience squirm! Suitably chastised by Jeremy Northam as Mr. Knightley, Emma at last starts to see the error of her rather selfish ways.

Persuasion 1995
BBC/Sony Drama

Director: Roger Michell
Producers: Fiona Finlay and
George Faber
Screenplay: Nick Dear

Starring: Amanda Root
Ciaran Hinds
Corin Redgrave
Susan Fleetwood
Sophie Thompson
Fiona Shaw

" Captain Wentworth perhaps has even more to attract his female audience than Mr. Darcy "

When Jane Austen wrote 'Persuasion' in 1815/16, she was battling against ill health. The novel was published posthumously in 1818.

Maturity and experience appear to have put greater understanding and depth into her writing and the reader is led to feel that there is something of Jane Austen's own life within the novel.

The television production of the book was excellent and the actors and actresses superbly cast. The mental cruelty inflicted on Anne Elliot by her unfeeling, self-centred family and the pain she feels as a result of her lost relationship with Captain Wentworth is tangible, thanks to the acting skills of Amanda Root. Captain Wentworth perhaps has even more to attract his female audience than Mr. Darcy.

Kellynch Hall, Somerset
Barnsley Park, Gloucestershire (Private Ownership. English Heritage Register)

Home of self-obsessed Sir Walter Elliot, "Vanity was the beginning and end of Sir Walter's character", and two of his daughters, Elizabeth and Anne.

Barnsley Park is an early 18th century house standing on the site of a medieval building. The house is of national significance and one of the finest Georgian houses in Gloucestershire.

Barnsley Park Village

Lyme Regis...
Plays itself. Well known for its starring role in John Fowles, 'The French Lieutenant's Woman', Lyme Regis is a charming Dorset seaside town. The town plays a prominent role in the novel 'Persuasion'. "The young people were all wild to see Lyme. Captain Wentworth talked of going there again himself; it was only seventeen miles from Uppercross."

Scenes of walks on the beach – part of Dorset's Jurassic Coast – and along the Cobb, where Louisa Musgrove has her near fatal fall, mirror the novel. "There was too much wind to make the high part of the new Cobb pleasant for the ladies, and they agreed to get down the steps to the lower, and all were contented to pass quietly and carefully down the steep flight, excepting Louisa; she must be jumped down them by Captain Wentworth."

Lyme Regis and the Dorset coast are simply beautiful. The long main street of the town dips down the hill towards the sea. At the top of the hill is the Mariners Hotel which was immortalised by Beatrix Potter in her children's book, 'The Tale of Little Pig Robinson.' The authoress spent a holiday in Lyme in 1904 and made drawings of the town to illustrate the book.

Author Henry Fielding also had a connection with the town. In 1725 he tried to run away with Sarah Andrew, the sixteen year old orphaned granddaughter and heiress of Solomon Andrew. Sarah's guardian disapproved of Henry Fielding's attentions and took her out of his reach. Allegedly she was the model for Sophia Western in Fielding's novel 'Tom Jones'.

Lyme Regis

Jane Austen stayed at Lyme Regis with her family in the summer of 1804. From the letters she wrote to her sister Cassandra we know that she spent her time walking on the Cobb, swimming from a bathing machine and dancing in the Assembly Rooms. The steps down from the Cobb, known as 'Granny's Teeth', are thought to have inspired the idea of Louisa's spirited but ill-judged attempted leap into Captain Wentworth's arms.

The Pump Room, Bath

Bath…

Plays itself. A large part of the novel is set in Bath whence the Elliot family move in order to make some economies. "Sir Walter would quit Kellynch Hall;- and after a very few days more of doubt and indecision, the great question of whither he should go was settled, and the first outline of this important change made out."

"There had been three alternatives, London, Bath or another house in the country. All Anne's wishes had been for the latter."

"But the usual fate of Anne attended her, in having something very opposite from her inclination fixed on. She disliked Bath, and did not think it agreed with her – and Bath was to be her home."

"Lady Russell was fond of Bath in short, and disposed to think it must suit them all."

Filming took place in several locations – the Roman Baths, the Pump Room and the Museum of Costume as well as around the streets. Bath provides film-makers with an authentic background of streets and buildings for films set in the Georgian era. The streets, the coffee houses, shops and meeting places all take the viewer back to Bath and the Georgian era.

The Assembly Rooms

All the main Assembly Rooms were used in the filming of 'Persuasion'. These rooms, opened in 1771, were purpose built for an 'assembly' – an 18th century entertainment. Large numbers of people

met together to see and be seen. They danced, drank tea, played cards, chatted, listened to music, walked about and flirted.

The Ballroom provided a very popular venue for dancing in the 18th century when balls for up to twelve hundred guests were held at least twice a week. Concerts were held in the Tea Room where refreshments were also served.

The Octagon and Card Room link the Ballroom and Tea Room. These rooms were originally designed as a space where guests could circulate, and they were also used for music and cards. On Sundays, cards were forbidden, but guests could instead listen to the organ, which stood in the musicians' gallery.

The Jane Austen Centre

Bath Tea Room

The Pump Room
There have been few changes to the Pump Room since Jane Austen's visits to the town. In the film Anne Elliot is seen taking the waters with Lady Russell, and hurrying across the rooms to greet Admiral and Mrs. Croft.

Museum of Costume
This is a museum of fashionable clothes illustrating the changing styles over the last four hundred years. Included in the displays are costumes from the late 18th and early 19th centuries similar to clothes worn by the characters in Jane Austen's books.

The Colonnades
Used in several scenes in the film, the Colonnades sheltered and framed Anne Elliot and Captain Wentworth for the kiss that never would have happened in 1815, but so surely was needed for the intensity of emotion that passed between these two charismatic central characters.

Nautical Scenes
Some of those shots of ships on the high seas are from a sequence from 'The Bounty', made by Paradise films in 1984.

The delightful costumes of the members of the Jane Austen Society

Sense and Sensibility 1995
Columbia/Mirage

Director: Ang Lee
Producer: Lindsay Doran
Screenplay: Emma Thompson

Starring: Emma Thompson
               Kate Winslet
               Hugh Grant
               Alan Rickman
               Hugh Laurie
               Robert Hardy
               Imelda Staunton
               Imogen Stubbs

The Locations

This 1995 film of 'Sense and Sensibility' was the second of Jane Austen's novels to be adapted for the big screen. Evicted from their home on the death of her husband (as women they could not inherit property), Mrs. Dashwood and her daughters remove to a cottage in Devon, where they are obliged to live on an income of five hundred pounds a year. With no status and no dowry, there is little hope of the girls making suitable marriages, or escaping from poverty. However, Marianne becomes enraptured by the dashing Mr. Willoughby, while caring intellectual Colonel Brandon has no hope....or does he? Elinor tries to ignore her feelings for Edward Ferrars but love triumphs in the end.

Norland Park
Saltram House, Plymouth, Devon
(National Trust)

"The family of Dashwood had been long settled in Sussex. The estate was large, and their residence was at Norland Park, in the centre of their property, where, for many generations, they had lived in so respectable a manner, as to engage the general good opinion of their surrounding acquaintance."

39

At Norland Park the stage is set for the action of the novel, as Mr. Henry Dashwood ends his days on earth. The second Mrs. Dashwood and her three daughters are forced from their home by the inheritor of the property, Mr. Dashwood's son from his first marriage, Mr John Dashwood and his avaricious wife. But greedy young Mrs. Dashwood has a brother, Mr. Edward Ferrars, who is of a decidedly different turn of mind and here at Norland Park feelings between Elinor and Edward are kindled.

The Dashwood girls, forced to leave Norland Park with their mother, travel to Devonshire to start life afresh in a new, but much reduced home.

Saltram House is an 18th century mansion built in the reign of George II. The house stands above the River Plym in a beautiful landscaped park. Visitors are treated to rooms designed by Robert Adams, considered as his greatest interior designs, original Chinese wallpapers and an incomparable collection of paintings, including works by Angelica Kauffman and Sir Joshua Reynolds.

Barton Cottage
Efford House, Flete Estate, Devon
(Private Ownership)

Flete Estate is a 5,000 acre estate not far from Plymouth. A number of secluded country cottages are available as holiday lets in this beautiful countryside on the south Devon coast.

Following an offer of a property by her relation Mr. John Middleton, Mrs. Dashwood and her three daughters made their home at Barton Cottage. "As a house, Barton Cottage, though small, was comfortable and compact; but as a cottage it was defective, for the building was regular, the roof was tiled, the window-shutters were not painted green, nor were the walls covered with honeysuckles."

Efford House is described by the Estate as 'A beautifully proportioned detached country house set in its own grounds bordered by mature woodlands'.

Playing the part of Barton Cottage, Efford House followed the specification precisely: "The situation of the house was good. High hills rose immediately behind, and at no greater distance on each side; some of which were open downs, the others cultivated and woody".

The Estate's description continues: 'With spectacular views across the higher reaches of the Erne, and a garden that stretches down to the

Efford House

40

edge of the estuary.' The spectacular coastal views shown in the film are an added extra not suggested by Jane Austen, and are available as part of a Devon holiday. All this and the chance to stay where Edward Ferrars (Hugh Grant) and Colonel Brandon (Alan Rickman) paid court to Elinor and Marianne Dashwood (Emma Thompson and Kate Winslet).

Barton Park
Trafalgar House Salisbury, Wiltshire (Private Ownership)

In 'Sense and Sensibility', the home of Sir John and Lady Middleton. "Barton Park was about half a mile away from the cottage." Mrs. Dashwood and her daughters were made merrily welcome by Sir John and his mother-in-law, Mrs. Jennings: "Mrs. Dashwood and her daughters were met at the door of the house by Sir John, who welcomed them to Barton Park with unaffected sincerity."

Trafalgar House is a Georgian property constructed of brick and stone. It was given to Lord Nelson's elder brother and closest male relative, the Reverend William Nelson. Formerly called Standlynch, the Estate was purchased by the Nation in 1814 and renamed 'Trafalgar' by an Act of Parliament. A short drive from the house is an Iron Age camp called Cherbury Ring.

Trafalgar House

Coombe Magna, Devon
Compton Castle (National Trust)

Lucky Mr. Willoughby to live in this fairy-tale castle, but maybe he was never allowed inside as the film only showed exterior shots! No wonder he liked his poetry though!

The castle was built as a fortified manor house between the 14th and 17th centuries by the Gilbert family. A descendant was Sir Humphrey Gilbert, half brother to Sir Walter Raleigh and coloniser of Newfoundland.

Fortified towers, battlements, buttresses, spiral staircases and minstrels' gallery – well worth a visit. A note to cooks, take a look at the Great Kitchen, which gives an idea of how it felt to be in the heat in medieval times. Also to be seen, chapels and churches and walled flower garden.

Mrs. Jennings' Town House Exterior
Mompesson House, Salisbury, Wiltshire (National Trust)

Mrs. Jennings takes Elinor and Marianne Dashwood to her London home for her annual January visit to London. The exterior shots were of Mompesson House, as were some of the interior scenes. "The house was handsome and handsomely fitted up."

Mompesson House is located at the heart of Salisbury in Cathedral Close, and offers a good example of Queen Anne architecture. A visit to the house includes admission to the charming walled garden laid out with pergola and traditional herbaceous borders.

Mompesson House

London Ballroom
Wilton House, Salisbury, Wiltshire
(National Trust)

Ten years before starring in the 2005 film adaptation of 'Pride and Prejudice', Wilton House featured in the filming of this earlier Jane Austen novel. Attending an assembly in London, which was shot in the Double Cube Room, Marianne Dashwood discovers Willoughby in a situation with Miss Grey, who is very rich. "Fifty thousand pounds, my dear. Did you ever see her? A smart, stylish girl they say, but not handsome."

Wilton House

Wilton House is the ancestral home of the Earl of Pembroke. The house, which has a fine collection of paintings, is open to the public, as are the gardens and parkland.

Cleveland, The Palmer Estate
Montacute House and Village, Somerset
(National Trust)

It is whilst visiting the Palmers' home, Cleveland, that Marianne Dashwood falls dangerously ill.

Montacute House

Montacute House is an Elizabethan mansion, and boasts the largest surviving Elizabethan long gallery in Britain, running one hundred and seventy two feet down the length of the building. The property houses collections of 17th and 18th century furniture and Elizabethan and Jacobean portraits.

Outside there are formal gardens with mixed borders and old roses, and the house is surrounded by a landscaped park.

The Brandons' Wedding
Berry Pomeroy, Devon

Here Marianne Dashwood and the delightful Colonel Brandon tied the knot. Oh sigh!

Berry Pomeroy Castle

Berry Pomeroy Church of St. Mary, standing a little under a mile from the ruins of Berry Pomeroy Castle is the delightful church where the wedding in 'Sense and Sensibility' was shot. Another country church in which to collect your thoughts and dwell upon women's lot in the early 19th century!

Pride and Prejudice 1995
BBC/A & E Mini-Series

Director: Simon Langton
Producer: Sue Birtwistle
Screenplay: Andrew Davies

Starring:

Jennifer Ehle
Colin Firth
Suzannah Harker
Julia Sawalha
Polly Maberly
Crispin
Bonham-Carter
Anna Chancellor
Adrian Lukis

Moving on to the acclaimed 1995 BBC production of 'Pride and Prejudice' and many a girl's favourite, Colin Firth as Mr. Darcy.

Adapted for television by Andrew Davies, the BBC mini-series held audiences captivated on Sunday evenings. An hour was always too short, and the week between episodes always too long! When the last episode drew to its satisfactory conclusion viewers knew that Sundays would never be quite the same again!!

The Locations

The Carriages
Red House Stables Working Carriage Museum, Darley Dale, near Matlock, Derbyshire

The emphasis here is on the 'working', although visitors are invited to look behind the scenes and meet the horses and ponies that work at the stables. Red House offers tours by coach and team of four horses or carriage and pair of horses around the Derbyshire countryside, including a trip to Chatsworth House, believed by many to have been the inspiration for Jane Austen's 'Pemberley'.

As well as 'Pride and Prejudice', Red House also supplied equipage for 'Sense and Sensibility' and 'Emma'.

Longbourn,
Home of The Bennets
Luckington Court, Luckington, Wiltshire (Private Ownership)

This attractive Georgian house, in a peaceful location away from the main road, provided a home for the Bennet family. Fake snow was liberally spread along the drive and round the gardens for the double wedding of Mr. Darcy and Lizzie Bennet and Mr. Bingley and Jane Bennet.

The 12th century church of St. Mary and St. Ethelbert also featured in the BBC production and the gardens of the Old Rectory were used as the Bennet's garden. The Old Rectory is also a private house, but offers bed and breakfast.

43

Lacock Village

Edgecote Hall

Teigh, Oakham

Meryton Town
Lacock, Wiltshire (National Trust)

Lacock is a 13th century village that has changed little over the years. Although cars line the streets, it is still possible to appreciate the location that was Meryton, where the younger Bennet girls giggled their way down the road on the look out for handsome young soldiers, and Lizzie had her first meeting with the calculating Wickham. The Red Lion was transformed for the film into Meryton's Assembly Rooms.

Netherfield Park Exterior
Edgecote Hall, Northamptonshire (Private Ownership)

The grand exterior of Edgecote Hall, with its dual staircases leading to the door, was shown as the Bennet family arrived at Mr. Bingley's ball. As it is a private house, let us move on, as the Bennets did, to the grand interior of Netherfield Park.

Mr. Bingley's Ballroom
Brocket Hall, Welwyn, Hertfordshire (Hotel)

The present Hall was built in the 18th century to the design of architect James Paine for its owner Sir Matthew Lamb. The ballroom is sixty feet long and features an Adam fireplace, Chippendale mirrors and ceilings painted by Sir Francis Wheatley. Sir Matthew's son became the first Lord Melbourne. Lady Caroline Lamb, wife of the second Lord Melbourne, had a brief love affair with Lord Byron, whom she described as 'mad, bad and dangerous to know'. She also had herself served up in a large soup tureen as a surprise dish for her husband's birthday. The fifty-four seater dining table around which the startled guests were seated still graces the room in this top conference and golfing hotel.

Mr. Collins' Parsonage
Teigh, Oakham, Rutland (Private Ownership)

A few miles from Oakham, in the pretty hamlet of Teigh, a private house was used as Mr. Collins' rectory. The house isn't open to the public, but it stands next to Holy Trinity church, which is of interest. The tower of the church is from the 13th and 14th centuries, but the interior is 18th century and remains much as it was when built in 1782. An unusual feature of the church is the location of the pulpit, which is at the back of the church. Worshippers must enter and leave the church beneath its floor.

Tea - the quintessential English tradition

Rosings, Home of
Lady Catherine de Bourgh
Belton House, Lincolnshire
(National Trust)

The approach to Belton House must have been less daunting for a young country girl than Burghley, nevertheless, Elizabeth must have felt overwhelmed by her first view of the BBC's version of Lady Catherine de Bourgh's stately residence. Mr. Collins, an obsequious companion, can only have made the situation worse as they walked up the imposing driveway.

Visitors today need not feel overawed. The house sits in beautiful parkland and delightful cultivated gardens. Belton is considered by many people to be the perfect English Country House. The Hondecoeter Room (named after the Dutch artist who painted the vast pictures) was the room used for the 'interviews' held by the formidable Lady Catherine de Bourgh and the adjacent room was the location for Elizabeth to play the piano. Mr. Darcy used the desk in the Blue Bedroom to write his explanatory letter to Elizabeth, and he was seen ascending the staircase to escape from the enquiries of his aunt. The curtains and the desk in the bedroom are those used in the production.

The house and its formal gardens, orangery, landscaped park and lakeside walk provide a pleasant day out.

Ramsgate
Weston-Super-Mare

Georgiana succumbed to Mr. Wickham's charms whilst taking the air in Ramsgate, but fortunately was plucked out of harm's way by Mr. Darcy before 'things had gone too far!' Not so with Lydia Bennet who eloped with the designing Mr. Wickham from Brighton whence she had gone with Colonel and Mrs. Forster in hot pursuit of the militiamen.

Pemberley, Darcy's Family Home
Exterior
Lyme Park, Disley, Stockport,
Cheshire (National Trust)

"…(Pemberley) situated on the opposite side of a valley, into which the road with some abruptness wound. It was a large, handsome, stone building, standing well on rising ground." "Elizabeth was delighted. She had never seen a place for which nature had done more, or where natural beauty had been so little counteracted by an awkward taste." The first view of Pemberley was shot from across the lake and park and gave the 'wow' factor needed to house Mr. Darcy in surroundings appropriate to his standing. Visitors may walk along the path and up the steps where Darcy and Elizabeth walked.

And the wet shirt lake scene? Sorry girls, Colin Firth, the man who climbed out, was not the man who dived in, and his swim took place in a specially designed tank!

Belton House Courtyard

Lyme Park

Pemberley Interiors I
Sudbury Hall, Sudbury, Near Ashbury,
Derbyshire (National Trust)

Several rooms were used at Sudbury Hall providing memorable scenes. The Long Gallery where Elizabeth and the Gardiners inspected Mr. Darcy's portrait with his housekeeper. The Grand Staircase, the Music Room and the Library where Darcy paid off Wickham after his attempted elopement with Georgiana, Mr. Darcy's young sister.

Sudbury Hall is a late 17th century house with gorgeous interiors, and includes wood carvings by Grinling Gibbons as well as painted ceilings and murals by Louis Laguerre.

London Coaching Inn
Lord Leycester Hospital, Warwick

These historic buildings provided the location for the bustling London scenes after Wickham had whisked Lydia away from the lackadaisical care of Colonel and Mrs. Forster.

These 14th century buildings were built at the behest of Thomas Beauchamp, 12th Earl of Warwick, and now present a pleasing half-timbered exterior and an impressive interior at the heart of Warwick. The hospital was reopened in the middle of the 20th century, and is now a self-supporting charity which relies for its income on visitors, who may also enjoy the delightfully restored Master's Garden and the Museum of the Queen's Own Hussars.

The hospital has also provided settings for 'Henry Fielding's novel, 'Tom Jones' and Daniel Defoe's 'Moll Flanders'.

Sudbury Hall - Pemberley

Lord Leycester Hospital, Warwick

Northanger Abbey

Northanger Abbey 1986
BBC/A & E Television Film

Director: Giles Foster
Producer: Louis Marks
Screenplay: Maggie Wadey

Starring: Katherine
               Schlesinger
               Peter Firth
               Robert Hardy
               Googie Withers
               Geoffrey Chater
               Cassie Stuart

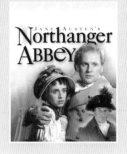

> " Catherine's wild imagination is fuelled at Northanger both by the Gothic setting and by her fantastic ideas surrounding the earlier death of Mrs. Tilney "

'Northanger Abbey' with its overtones of Gothic drama, was shot principally in Bath and at Bodiam Castle. The heroine, Catherine Morland, is a young teenager, prone to daydreaming and heavily influenced by the Gothic writings of Ann Radcliffe, author of 'The Romance of the Forest' and 'The Mysteries of Udolpho'.

"Her father was a clergyman, without being neglected, or poor, and a very respectable man." Catherine grew up in a small village, one of ten children, and she was rather plain. Invited by her neighbours, Mr. and Mrs. Allen to join them in Bath to be brought out into society, Catherine is overwhelmed with excitement and her fanciful mind creates a myriad Gothic romances, herself as the heroine. Whilst there, she meets the Tilney family and is invited to stay at Northanger Abbey.

Catherine's wild imagination is fuelled at Northanger both by the Gothic setting and by her fantastic ideas surrounding the earlier death of Mrs. Tilney.

The Locations

The Morlands' Home
Corsham Court, Wiltshire
(Private Ownership)

The film opens with Catherine Morland ensconced in a tree, a copy of a Gothic novel open in her lap. She daydreams of kidnap by evil 'barons' and rescue by gallant 'knights' – scenes enacted and brought to life as her dreams within the action of the film.

Corsham Court, an Elizabethan house, appears fleetingly in the film.

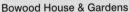
Bowood House & Gardens

The State Rooms house a collection of over one hundred and fifty paintings, statuary, bronzes and furniture. Chippendale, Van Dyck, the Adam Brothers, Rubens, Reynolds and Romney are all represented, plus a piano by Clementi.

Outside, the extensive 'Capability' Brown gardens and landscape include a lake, specimen trees and herbaceous borders.

Bath
The Pump-room

The Pump-room, the place to 'see and be seen' in fashionable Bath. "With more than usual eagerness did Catherine hasten to the Pump-room the next day, secure within herself of seeing Mr. Tilney there before the morning were over."

The Roman Baths

Catherine Morland joins her friends to swim in the health promoting waters. This scene seems truly bizarre, and does not feature in the novel. Many of the characters who have already been introduced to the audience wade about in the waters wearing brown costumes, and trays around their necks. These trays never seem to be used for anything, but the characters wade around as in a ritual slow dance.

Other settings in Bath include the Royal Crescent and the Colonnades, which seem a popular film location for characters to meet within the frame of the pillars.

Temple and Waterfall
Bowood House and Gardens, Calne
(The Marquis of Lansdowne)

When Catherine Morland finally gets away for her walk with the Tilney siblings, they are seen walking around Bath, finishing their walk at a waterfall as the skies open. This waterfall is the cascade at Bowood House where the Doric temple is also shown. "The Tilneys called for her at the appointed time.....They determined on walking round Beechen Cliff, that noble hill, whose beautiful verdure and hanging coppice render it so striking an object from almost every opening in Bath."

Bowood is an early 18th century house, which was decreased in size after demolition of part of the structure in 1955. The Diocletian wing houses a library and a laboratory where Joseph Priestley discovered oxygen gas in 1774.

On display in the house are collections of watercolours, miniatures, jewellery and Georgian costumes, including Lord Byron's Albanian dress.

The house is set in 2,000 acres of gardens and grounds that were landscaped by 'Capability' Brown in the latter half of the 18th century.

Northanger Abbey
Bodiam Castle, Bodiam, near
Robertsbridge, East Sussex
(The National Trust)

Brooding Bodiam was the ideal Gothic setting for 'Northanger Abbey' in the 1986 television production of Jane Austen's novel. The novel, which is intentionally witty, is a spoof on the Gothic literature of Jane Austen's era.

Catherine Morland goes to stay with her new friends, the Tilneys, at Northanger Abbey, eager for a first sighting of their home: "As they drew near the end of their journey, her impatience for a sight of the abbey – for some time suspended by his (Mr. Tilney's) conversation on subjects very different – returned in full force, and every bend in the road was expected with solemn awe to afford a glimpse of its massy walls of grey stone, rising amidst a grove of ancient oaks, with the last beams of the sun playing on its high Gothic windows. But so low did the building stand that she found herself passing through the great gates of the lodge into the very grounds of Northanger, without having discerned even an antique chimney."

The film-makers chose Bodiam Castle as Northanger Abbey, which fulfilled Catherine's fantastical ideas, but was perhaps not quite as Jane Austen's description in the novel. "The windows, to which she looked with peculiar dependence, from having heard the General talk of his preserving them in their Gothic form with reverential care,

Bodiam Castle

were yet less what her fancy had portrayed. To be sure, the pointed arch was preserved – the form of them was Gothic – they might be even casements – but every pane was so large, so clear, so light!"

Built in 1385 as a defence for the surrounding Sussex countryside, Bodiam Castle is one of the finest examples of medieval architecture in the country. The exterior of the castle gives an impression of completeness, but inside it is a ruin, although, some of the floors have been replaced in the towers, allowing visitors to climb the spiral staircases for spectacular views of the Rother valley and local steam trains. Visitors may also explore the romantic castle grounds and in the museum, learn more of Bodiam's fascinating past.

Pride and Prejudice 1940
MGM Feature Film

Director: Robert Z. Leonard
Producer: Hunt Stromberg
Screenplay: Aldous Huxley
Jane Murfin

Starring: Greer Garson
Laurence Olivier
Maureen O'Sullivan
Ann Rutherford
Mary Boland
Edmund Gwenn

> " Cedric Gibbons spent two years in England tracking down authentic Georgian props with no expense spared "

The Locations

MGM Studios Back Lot

Whilst every production of a Jane Austen novel is not included in this book, it is appropriate that the one that started it all is given a mention.

The 1940 production of 'Pride and Prejudice' was made at the MGM Studios in America using a screenplay written by Aldous Huxley and Jane Murfin. Whilst there are no locations to see in England, an interesting snippet of information was provided in an interview with Kenneth Turan by Ann Rutherford. She observed that Cedric Gibbons spent two years in England tracking down authentic Georgian props with no expense spared. Unfortunately, no one had informed him that a decision had been taken back at MGM to change the costumes to those of the Victorian era with the result that the large, hooped dresses were too cumbersome for the props, many of which were broken.

The enterprising lady, recognising the value of some of the artefacts, which included pieces of Meissen, retrieved the broken pieces from the rubbish where it had been deposited by the prop man!

Greer Garson & Laurence Olivier

51

Jane Austen was born in the Rectory on 16th December 1775 at Steventon near Basingstoke. She was the younger of two girls who had five older brothers and one younger. The Reverend George Austen was an enlightened father who encouraged Jane in her literary pursuits, and she read much, including works by Henry Fielding, Laurence Sterne and Samuel Richardson.

The rectory at Steventon is no longer standing, but pay a visit to the Church of St. Nicholas where there are many connections with Jane Austen. The spire would have been unknown to Jane having been added to the church in Victorian times. Look out for the weather vane on the Church which is now in the form of a quill pen in memory of the village's famous daughter. When Jane was only seven, she and her older sister, Cassandra, were sent away to boarding school in Oxford. When the school moved to Southampton the sisters went too, but the establishment was suddenly disbanded owing to an outbreak of what was termed 'the putrid sore throat'. After the girls had recovered they were again sent away, this time to Reading where they attended a school in the gatehouse of the old abbey.

In 1801, the Reverend George Austen, Jane's father retired with his family to Bath and Jane's feelings on this move are reflected in those of Anne Elliot in Persuasion: "dreading the possible heats of September in all the white glare of Bath, and grieving to forego all the influence, so sweet and so sad, of the autumnal months in the country."

Jane accepted a proposal of marriage from Harris Bigg-Wither in December 1802, but after a sleepless night of reflection rescinded her acceptance on the following morning.

Following her husband's death in 1805, Jane's mother moved with her daughters and son Frank to Southampton, they moved to their new home in Chawton. The house was provided by Jane's brother, Edward, who had inherited the estate of Thomas Knight by whom he had been adopted. Jane had been a regular visitor at the Knight's home, Godmersham Park. The house at Chawton is now a museum dedicated to Jane Austen, where the parlour is shown as the place where she wrote 'Mansfield Park', 'Emma' and 'Persuasion.' Jane wrote her novels with family life continuing around her, but she still wrote rather secretively, hiding her works in progress from visitors to the house.

Jane Austen was moved to 8, College Street, Winchester to be near her physician, but died, most probably from Addisons Disease, in July 1817 with Cassandra at her side. At the time of her death Jane was working on a new novel, 'Sanditon' which was never completed.

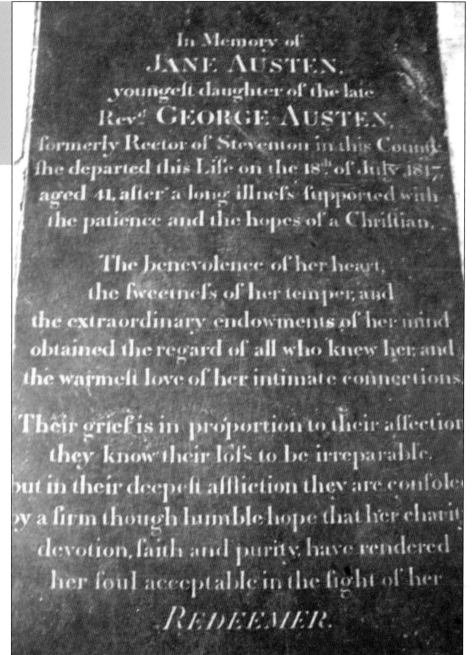

Jane Austen's Tombstone

She was buried on 24th July in the North Aisle at Winchester Cathedral and her tomb is marked with the inscription:

In Memory of
Jane Austen
Younger daughter of the late
Revd George Austen
formerly Rector of Steventon in this
County
she departed this Life on 18th of July
1817
aged 41, after a long illness
supported with
the patience and the hopes of a
Christian

The benevolence of her heart,
the sweetness of her temper, and
the extraordinary endowments of her
mind
obtained the regard of all who knew
her, and
the warmest love of her intimate
connections

Their grief is in proportion to their
affection
they know their loss to be
irreparable,
but in their deepest affliction they are
consoled
by a firm though humble hope that
her charity
devotion, faith and purity have
rendered
her soul acceptable in the sight of her
REDEEMER

A guide was amused some years ago to be asked where 'Barbara Cartland' was buried. Much bemused, she tried to assure the lady that Mrs. Cartland was alive and well, but to no avail. After much fruitless searching the visitor remembered that it was in fact Jane Austen's tomb that she was seeking. One wonders how much of a literary connection there is between the two authors for the confusion to have arisen?!

Jane Austen's Bath and the
Jane Austen Centre
…a must for any fan of the authoress.

Jane Austen had strong links with Bath, a city which she visited in 1797 and 1799, and where she lived from 1801 – 1805. In two of her novels, 'Northanger Abbey' and 'Persuasion', Bath is central to the plots, and all of her novels mention the city.

Jane Austen moved, with her mother, father and sister to Bath in 1801, and her father died in the city at Green Park Buildings. He is buried at St. Swithins at Walcot, Bath, and there is a memorial in the church grounds, which is well visited by Austen fans, who make the trek along the Paragon to see his tombstone.

Rev. George Austen

Rev. George Austen's tombstone

The Jane Austen Centre, located at 40, Gay Street, was opened to celebrate the life of the city's most famous resident. The Centre, which has a Georgian shop front, offers visitors an introductory talk, Georgian costumes made from authentic fabrics and a specially commissioned film starring Amanda Root. At the Centre, visitors find out about the writer, the characters and settings of her novels, and a great deal about Regency life, society, dress and manners. 'Walking Tours of Jane Austen's Bath' are led by experienced guides who take visitors to the places where Jane lived, walked and shopped, and to the places made famous in her Bath novels. These walks are held every weekend, and every September there is a nine-day 'Jane Austen festival', involving food, music, drama, tours, costume, lecture and film, which attracts an audience from around the world.

The friendly and helpful Jane Austen Centre staff

The Jane Austen Centre

Whilst residing in Bath, Jane lived at several addresses - Green Park Buildings; 25, Gay Street; Trim Street, and, for the most part at 4, Sydney Place. The part of Green Park Buildings where she resided with her family was bombed during the Second World War and no longer stands.

When Jane Austen was moved from Steventon to Bath, she was uprooted from her settled country life, and she found it difficult to adapt to the city. Whilst Bath was inspirational for her, she had little time for writing, and the family library and piano had to be sold. The death of her father in the city must also have increased her reputed dislike of Bath. However, her legacy to the city is great, and it is thanks to her writing that people the world over have become familiar with the city landscapes and buildings. This urban landscape, now a World Heritage Site, survives today to provide enjoyment for the many, many people who visit the city and walk in the footsteps of Jane Austen.

The Jane Austen Centre receives over 40,000 visitors each year and sells almost 50,000 of her books!

The Jane Austen House Museum, Chawton

1787-93 Comic essays, skits and short stories written, later copied into three manuscript books entitled Volumes the First, Second and Third. Now referred to as her Juvenilia and not published in her lifetime.

1793-94 'Lady Susan written, but never published in her lifetime.

1795 'Elinor and Marianne' written, revised 1797-98 and 1809 into 'Sense and Sensibility'.

1796-97 'First Impressions' written, revised 1811-12 into 'Pride and Prejudice.

1797-98 'Susan' written, revised 1803 and 1816; renamed 'Northanger Abbey' when published.

1803 With her brother Henry's assistance, the manuscript and copyright of 'Susan' was sold for £10.00 to the publisher Crosby & Co., advertised but never brought out.

1804 'The Watsons' started, but never completed.

1811 'Sense and Sensibility' by 'A Lady' published by Egerton.

1811-13 'Mansfield park' written.

1813 'Pride and Prejudice' by the author of 'Sense and Sensibility' published.

1814 'Mansfield Park' published by Egerton.

1814-15 'Emma' written.

1816 'Emma' published by Murray. The novel is dedicated to HRH Prince Regent. This same year, Jane's brother Henry, using subterfuge, buys the manuscript and copyright of the unpublished 'Susan' for £10.00.

1815-16 'Persuasion' written and completed in July 1816 when Jane's health was deteriorating.

1817 'Sanditon' started and twelve chapters written, but never completed.

1818 'Susan' now renamed 'Northanger Abbey' and 'Persuasion' published posthumously.

Jane Austen by Mellissa Dring

Jane Austen's Britain

Ireland - *County Meath,* *Higginsbrook House, near Trim, Steventon Rectory, B J*
County Offaly, *Charleville Castle, Tullamore, Lady Gresham's Home, B J*
Dublin, *City Hall, The Ballroom, B J*
Dublin, *Henrietta Street and King's Inn, Regency London, B J*
Dublin Castle, *Henrietta Street and King's Inn, Bath & Regency London, B J*
County Wicklow, *Killruddery House, Bray, Lady Gresham's Home, B J*
County Waterford, *Lismore Castle, Northanger Abbey*

Cheshire - *Stockport,* *Lyme Park, Pemberley, P & P 1995*

Derbyshire - *Bakewell,* *Chatsworth House, Pemberley Exterior, P & P 2005*
Hathersage Moor, *Stanage Edge, P & P 2005*
Bakewell, *Haddon Hall, The Inn at Lambton & Elizabeth Bennet's Bedroom, P & P 2005*
Bakewell, *The Rutland Arms Hotel, Life*
Matlock, *Red House Carriages, Darley Dale, Supplied Horses and Carriages, P & P 1995 / S & S / Emma*
Ashbury, *Sudbury Hall, Pemberley Interior 1, P & P 1995*

Warwickshire - *Warwick,* *Lord Leycester Hospital, London Coaching Inn, P & P 1995*

Gloucestershire - *Cheltenham,* *Sudeley Castle, Donwell Abbey, Emma TV 1996*
Winchcombe, *Stanway House & Water Garden, Donwell Abbey Interior, Emma TV 1996*
Barnsley Park, *Kellynch Hall, Persuasion*

Somerset - *East Coker,* *Church, Emma Film 1996*
Bath, *Bath, Northanger Abbey, Persuasion, S & S*
Bath, *Jane Austen's Home, Life*
Montacute, *Montacute House and Village, Cleveland, S & S*
Weston-Super-Mare Seaside, *Ramsgate, P & P 1995*

Devon - *Plymouth,* *Saltram House, Norland Park, S & S 1995*
Flete Estate, *Efford House, Barton Cottage, S & S 1995*
Compton Castle, *Combe Magna, S & S 1995*
Berry Pomeroy, *The Brandons, Wedding, S & S 1995*
Hartland Abbey Estate, *Blackpool Mill Cottage
and Coastal Footpath, S & S 2008*

Cornwall - *Charlestown,* *Mansfield Park 1999*

Dorset - *Coastal Views,* *Mansfield Park 1999*
Evershot, *Highbury, Emma Film 1996*
Milton Abbas, *Home of Lizzie the pig, Emma 1996*
Beaminster, *Mapperton House, Weddings, puppies and pergolas, Emma Film 1996*
Countryside, *Box Hill, Emma film 1996*
Lyme Regis, *Lyme Regis, Persuasion & Persuasion 2007*
Seatown, *Meeting on the beach, Persuasion 2007*

Wiltshire - *Inn at Lyme Regis,* *Great Chalfield Manor, Persuasion 2007*

North Yorkshire - *Ripon,* *Newby Hall, Mansfield Park 2007*

Lincolnshire - *Stamford,* *Meryton, P & P 2005*
Stamford, *Burghley House, Rosings, P & P 2005*
Belton House, *Rosings, P & P 1995*

Rutland - *Oakham,* *St Peter's Church*
Brooke, *Mr. Collins' Church Interior, P & P 2005*
Oakham, *House, Teigh, Mr Collins' Parsonage, P & P 1995*

Northampton - *Corby,* *Kirby Hall, Mansfield Park, Mansfield Park*
Edgecote Hall, *Netherfield Exterior, P & P 1995*

Oxfordshire - *Banbury,* *Broughton Castle, Donwell Abbey, Emma TV 1996*
Thame Park, *Abbey Mill Farm, Emma 1996 TV*

Buckinghamshire - *Middle Claydon,* *Donwell Abbey, Emma Film 1996*
Beaconsfield, *Hall Barn, S & S 2008*

Berkshire - *Reading,* *Basildon Park, Lower Basildon, Netherfield, P & P 2005*
Windsor, *Dorney Court, Randalls, Emma TV 1996*
Reading, *City Gate, School, Jane Austen's Life*

Middlesex - *Isleworth,* *Osterley Park House, Visit to stately home, Mansfield Park*

London - *Hampstead,* *Kenwood House, Gardens, Mansfield Park*

Kent - *Tunbridge Wells,* *Richmond Place, Longbourn, P & P 2005*
Goudhurst, *Finchcocks Musical Instrument Museum, Loan of Instruments,*
P & P 2005 / Emma Film 1996 / S & S 1995

Surrey - *Richmond,* *Ham House, S & S 2008*
Guildford, *Loseley Park, S & S 2008*

Sussex - *Robertsbridge,* *Bodiam Castle, Northanger Abbey, Northanger Abbey*

Hampshire - *Portsmouth,* *Mansfield Park*
Basingstoke, *Steventon, Jane Austen's Birthplace, Life*
Southampton, *Jane and Cassandra Austen's School*
Home, *later, Life*
Chawton, *Austens' home, Life*
Winchester, *8 College Street, Home and where Jane Austen died, Life*
Winchester, *Cathedral, Jane Austen's Grave, Life*

Wiltshire - *Salisbury,* *Wilton House,*
Pemberley Interior, P & P 2005
Stourton, *Temple of Apollo, Stourhead*
Gardens, Rosings gardens, P & P 2005
Lacock, *Highbury, Emma, TV 1996 /*
P & P 1995
Trafalgar House, *Hartfield, Emma, TV 1996*
Salisbury, *Trafalgar House, Barton Park,*
S & S 1995
Salisbury, *Mompesson House,*
Mrs Jennings, Town House, S & S 1995
Luckington, *Luckington Court,*
Longbourn, P & P 2005
Corsham Court, *The Morland's Home,*
Northanger Abbey 1986
Calne, *Bowood House and Gardens,*
Temples and waterfall, Northanger Abbey
Sheldon Manor, *Chippenham, Persuasion 2007*

With Grateful Thanks

Grateful thanks to Dr. Karen Pusey and Mrs. Mavis Palfreman for their support and assistance in writing this book, and for the patience and understanding of my husband, Dennis.

Whilst gathering material for the book I met some very helpful and kind people, and special thanks goes to the staff at Kirby Hall, and the people at The Wheatsheaf in Oakham who greeted me with cheer, rustled up lunch after the kitchen had closed and provided a relaxing hour in their sunny beer garden.

Marcia Kennedy-McLuckie

Research and Images
Credits and Sources

www.workingtitlefilms.com

Hudson's Historic Houses and Gardens

Rutland and Stamford Mercury

Stamford Museum

Oakham Museum

Cityscape Maps Limited

www.janeausten.co.uk

www.pemberley.com

The Jane Austen Centre, Bath

Lucy Worsley – Inspector of Ancient monuments and Historic Buildings

St. Peter's, Brooke.
A History and Guide

www.le.ac.uk/emoha/leicester/teigh

Anthony Finney at
www.sndc.demon.co.uk/japp.htm

The Shell Guide to England edited by John Hadfield

Western Daily Press

www.lymeregismuseum.co.uk

www.devon.gov.uk
www.dicamillocompanion.com/houses

www.jasna.org

The Making of Pride and Prejudice

The Making of Jane Austen's Emma

The National Trust
www.nationaltrust.org

English Heritage

Debbie Lewis at Stanway House

Ros Liddington at Wilton House
Pg 8 image reproduced by kind permission of the Earl of Pembroke and the Trustees of the Wilton Estate

The Richard Burnett Collection Finchcocks Musical Museum

The curators and owners of all the locations featured in this book for their assistance and co-operation

Printed in England Ref No: 060152
www.trailpublishing.co.uk